TOP TIPS

FOR

GROOMS

James Harrison

summersdale

TOP TIPS FOR GROOMS

Copyright © Summersdale Publishers Ltd, 2014

Research by Sarah Herman

Decorations © Invisible Studio/Shutterstock.com

An Hachette UK Company
www.hachette.co.uk

Summersdale Publishers Ltd
Part of Octopus Publishing Group Limited
Carmelite House
50 Victoria Embankment
LONDON
EC4Y 0DZ
UK

www.summersdale.com

Printed and bound in the Czech Republic

ISBN: 978-1-84953-536-6

Substantial discounts on bulk quantities of Summersdale books are available to corporations, professional associations and other organisations. For details contact general enquiries: telephone: +44 (0) 1243 771107 or email: enquiries@summersdale.com.

CONTENTS

INTRODUCTION.............................4

THE NIGHT BEFORE.........................6

WAKEY-WAKEY!...........................23

LOOKING GOOD............................38

GROOMLY GREETINGS...................52

POMP AND CEREMONY...................65

SAY CHEESE!...............................81

A GRAND RECEPTION.....................95

TOASTS AND CAKE........................110

PARTY TIME...............................127

HONEYMOONERS..........................143

INTRODUCTION

Congratulations! You're getting married and the big day is fast approaching. Compared to the proposal, you probably think getting married will be a breeze. And, as exciting and fun as it is, the planning can be time-consuming, stressful and nerve-wracking (if not for you, then definitely for your bride). The wedding day, however, should be none of these things. It should be exciting, exhilarating and ever-so-slightly emotional, filled with love and laughter, and ending with a party to end all parties.

Being a groom is never as simple as just showing up. Even if you weren't involved in the planning, there are plenty of ways you can dodge disaster, impress your bride and contribute to the success of the wedding on the day. This book is the holy grail of groom guidance and it's got you covered from the night before you say 'I do!' right up until the honeymoon suite, where you will probably be equally as agreeable. So put the champagne on ice, call your bestest of men and prepare to enjoy the most wonderful, worry-free wedding day of your life.

THE NIGHT BEFORE

After years of living the single dream, then dating the girl of your dreams, tomorrow is the day you say 'I do' to a real lifetime of love. Get your head in the game and think like a pro-footballer the night before the big match to avoid getting blotto or sleeping in.

THE RIGHT MINDSET

Get your silliness out of your system. Tomorrow is a very important day with serious implications. Yes, it should be fun, but unless your bride-to-be is marrying you specifically for your fart jokes, it's a good idea to de-silly yourself the night before. Hang out with mates, watch your favourite comedy show and start giggling. It will also help you to relax and give those abs a workout.

Don't worry, just relax...
Enjoy the roses and
breathe them in; enjoy each
moment that you live.

TIFFANY ALVORD

THE LAST SUPPER

You're not spending your last night on death row before facing Ol' Sparky, so don't treat your last unmarried dinner as an opportunity to expand your waistline. You might not care if your breath still smells of garlic or if you spend your wedding day excusing yourself because of a dodgy curry the night before, but your bride certainly will.

LAST-MINUTE PREPERATION

◇ If you're feeling nervous, that's perfectly normal. Talk through any worries you might have with a close mate or relative and you'll soon realise you're just really, really excited!

◇ Read through your wedding vows if you've written them yourself (or write them if you've left it to the last minute!) – it will help to refocus your mind on what the whole day is going to be about. Similarly, take a look over your wedding speech to make sure you remember to thank everyone.

◇ Cut all the tags off any new clothes that you or your groomsmen are going to be wearing, and make sure everything is pressed to perfection.

◇ Try not to call your spouse-to-be; it will make the grand reveal of seeing them the next day all the more special. If you can't resist, send them a special message to tell them how you feel.

DON'T FORGET...

Spend 30 minutes or so going through your wedding checklist of all the items you need to remember for the next day. Make sure you know where the following things are located:

◇ Your full wedding-day outfit, whether that be a traditional suit (two or three pieces) with shirt and tie/cravat, or a kilt, a kimono, or a T-shirt and shorts

◇ Accessories (cufflinks, handkerchief, braces, hat, etc.)

◇ Buttonhole (is this being delivered the following day or are you getting it at the venue?)

◇ Shoes (with accompanying socks)

◇ Underpants (if you have a lucky pair then make sure they're clean!)

◇ The wedding rings

◇ Wallet and other personal items (phone, etc.)

◇ Jacket and an umbrella, just in case

◇ Any other items, e.g. any alternative clothing, wedding vows, wedding speech, any gifts (e.g. for the groomsmen, flower girls, etc.).

It's OK to have butterflies in your stomach. Just get them to fly in formation.

ROB GILBERT

*You know you're in love
when you can't fall asleep
because reality is finally
better than your dreams.*

DR SEUSS

SLEEP LIKE A KING

Getting a good night's sleep before the big day will make sure you look and feel your best the next day. Don't let butterflies get the better of you with these sleep-tastic tips.

◇ Get in a good workout at some point during the day. That way your muscles will feel relaxed and ready to rest.

◇ Wind down early by chilling out however you choose after dinner.

◇ Turn the lights down low and sip on a cup of camomile tea or warm milk (go on, we won't judge). Failing that, a shot of your best whisky will do the trick.

◇ Take a hot shower.

◇ If you can, avoid relying on sleeping pills or drinking too much alcohol – these could affect you negatively the next day.

DISASTER
DODGER

While it should take you less time to get ready than your beautiful bride, you don't want to be feeling rushed tomorrow. Make sure you set an alarm, giving yourself more than enough time to be able to enjoy your last morning of unwedded bliss. Remember, being late to the ceremony is only the prerogative of the bride.

Thank God for all I missed,
because it led me here to this.

<small>DARIUS RUCKER</small>

*A good marriage is like
a casserole, only those
responsible for it really
know what goes in it.*

Anonymous

YOUR NOTES

....
....
....
....
....
....
....
....
....
....
....
....
....
....

YOUR NOTES

....
....
....
....
....
....
....
....
....
....
....
....
....
....
....

WAKEY-WAKEY!

Like a kid on Christmas morning, you're waking up to a day of marvellous magic. Keep your cool, go with the flow and don't get your knickers in a twist. This morning is all about relaxing and prepping yourself for your partner.

A LITTLE HELP

Your groomsmen made sure your stag-do was one you'll probably never be able to fully remember. Now's the time to make sure they help you deliver a day you'll never forget. Unmarried mates will be a bit bewildered by what you're about to do, and married ones will know what's going through your groomy mind, so harness their help and support to make sure things run smoothly.

BREAKFAST OF CHAMPIONS

Before any fun and frolics take place, your stomach and the hardy tummies of your bestest men need lining. Prepare a plentiful fry-up feast with all the trimmings before any Dutch courage comes your way and you're guaranteed to make it to the ceremony with a full platoon of suited and booted buddies.

SETTING THE MOOD

◇ The morning will have been planned with the bride's lengthy beautifying requirements in mind. Don't get dressed too soon, otherwise you'll end up with a baked beans stain on your crisp white shirt.

◇ Have a drink *before* you get to the ceremony venue – there's nothing as unclassy as a gentlemanly groom standing outside a church holding a beer can.

◇ Get the party started with your favourite tunes or play some video games with the guys to keep the mood relaxed.

When you arise in the morning, think of what a precious privilege it is to be alive – to breathe, to think, to enjoy, to love.

MARCUS AURELIUS

DON'T FORGET...

It's OK to be romantic. If your bride's given you a little gift or card to open on the day, don't be embarrassed to do it in front of your mates. If anything, it will help them better understand why you're saying goodbye to your bachelor days. Likewise, why not do one of the following to make her smile before she sees you:

◇ Send her a 'Happy Wedding Day!' text message or a photograph of your wedding breakfast!

◇ Leave a card with some romantic words about the day in her handbag.

◇ Buy her a piece of jewellery or some sexy underwear she can wear on the day, and have her maid of honour give it to her in the morning.

◇ Organise for a horse and carriage or a fancy car to pick her up for the wedding (especially if she thought she was going in a taxi).

A CLOSE SHAVE

If you're planning on being baby-smooth for the big day, make sure you get up in good time for a hot, steamy soak to open up those pores.

By shaving earlier in the morning there'll be more time for any redness to go down and ample opportunities for your groomsmen to tell you if you missed a spot.

◇ Don't try a new shaving regime on the day – this is something you should have planned in advance.

◇ If you're feeling shaky with nerves, wait to shave – you don't want to look like you've lost a fight to a razor blade.

◇ Slap on the moisturiser afterwards to avoid a rash and to leave your skin smelling divine.

*Happily ever after is not
a fairy tale. It's a choice.*

Fawn Weaver

One word frees us of all the weight and pain of life: That word is love.

SOPHOCLES

DISASTER DODGER

If you're not staying at your own house, do a second check first thing in the morning to make sure you have everything you need and that your groomsmen are fully kitted out. If you realise early enough that something is missing, you can send a mate out to pick it up (a pair of matching socks, for example) – but leave it until five minutes before you're due to leave and someone's definitely going to have cold feet.

Enjoy the little things in life… For one day you'll look back and realise they were the big things.

KURT VONNEGUT

YOUR NOTES

....

....

....

....

....

....

....

....

....

....

....

....

....

....

YOUR NOTES

....
....
....
....
....
....
....
....
....
....
....
....
....
....

LOOKING GOOD

*While it's true that more eyes
are on the bride at a wedding,
that's usually because the groom
looks so polished that he doesn't
detract from her glamorous
gown and cascading hair-do.
Fall short by even a bit and all
anyone will be looking at is your
greasy hair, dirty shoes or missing
cufflinks. Here's how to wow.*

*The earth is like a
beautiful bride who needs
no manmade jewels to
heighten her loveliness.*

KAHLIL GIBRAN

SUITS YOU

◇ Make sure your outfit has been pressed professionally at the drycleaners and is hung covered and uncrushed in a wardrobe. Let the suit breathe the night before and press any outstanding creases carefully if required. Don't go crazy with a hot iron and ruin your brand new suit. A crease always trumps a burn hole. Tell your groomsmen to do the same, especially if you've splashed out on suits for them.

◇ It's all in the details – a shirt that fits and sits flat against your body, a quality silk handkerchief, a pair of bright orange socks that tie in with the flower arrangements. Don't leave anything to chance by assuming it will all look OK on the day. Invite your buddies round for beers and try on your outfits the week before the wedding so you're confident everything ties together as you imagined.

LOOKING SHARP

◇ Keep your shirt in place with braces (or tuck the tails into your pants for that taut appearance).

◇ Make sure you've clipped and cleaned your nails (especially if you're going to wear a wedding ring) and that you've addressed any facial manscaping, paying particular attention to errant nose and ear hairs!

◇ Don't put your jacket on until you reach the ceremony to avoid creasing the back of it on the sofa at home or in the car.

◇ Brush your teeth before you leave the house.

◇ Make sure you leave enough time to have a few photographs taken before you leave for the ceremony.

*The most beautiful things
in the world cannot be seen
or even touched; they must
be felt with the heart.*

HELEN KELLER

SPIT AND POLISH

If you've never been to a regimental private school or joined the army, polishing your shoes is something you might rarely do. Expensive leather shoes – the kind of which you might have purchased precisely for this occasion – require the utmost respect and attention. Take note…

Tools:
2 x quality brushes (one stiff, one softer), a cloth duster, and wax polish that matches the colour of your shoes (obvious, but a likely mistake!), shoe trees or newspaper

Steps:

1. Take out the shoelaces and clean any obvious dirt off the shoes – this can be done with a damp cloth.

2. Put in shoe trees (or some scrunched up newspaper) to stretch out the shoes.

3. Using the cloth or the stiff brush, apply a small amount of polish in circular motions to the whole shoe, including the tongue and heel.

4. Leave for 20 minutes for the leather to absorb the polish.

5. Buff using the softer brush and your biceps!

6. Pop the shoes on and buff again using the cloth in a sawing motion for a spectacular shine.

DON'T FORGET...
BITS AND BUTTONHOLES

◇ As uninterested as you might have been in picking out the wedding flowers, your buttonholes will make the groomsmen's outfits so don't forget to remind everyone to put them on.

◇ If you're not great at fiddly jobs, ask someone else to fix your buttonhole for you as they are delicate and can easily be damaged.

◇ Make sure the groomsmen's ties/cravats and handkerchiefs are neatly positioned to avoid looking scruffy.

◇ Sentimental cufflinks (such as your father's or grandfather's) make a great finish to a dress shirt. Don't finish off your polished outfit with cheap cracker cufflinks.

*I think men who have
a pierced ear are better
prepared for marriage.
They've experienced pain
and bought jewellery.*

RITA RUDNER

DISASTER DODGER

If you are inclined to wear a little fake tan on your big day, you must plan this into your schedule for the few days leading up to the wedding, otherwise there's a good chance your bright white shirt will end up with tan stains – not to mention your bride's outfit. Use a tried-and-tested product and give it a few days to settle. Remember not to go overboard – your bride will want to be the one emitting a beautiful glow, not you.

YOUR NOTES

....
....
....
....
....
....
....
....
....
....
....
....
....
....
....

YOUR NOTES

....
....
....
....
....
....
....
....
....
....
....
....
....
....
....

GROOMLY
GREETINGS

As the groom, you have the pleasure of arriving at the ceremony venue first, settling into your surroundings, greeting the officiant and some of your guests, and setting the tone for the day. These tips will help you to make the most of those precious moments before your bride appears.

MEETING AND GREETING

Don't be shy. More than anything weddings are truly their best when all the guests feel relaxed and like one big happy family. This comes largely from how the bride and groom react. When you see guests arriving at the venue, greet them, smile and wave. Even if you don't know someone, they are probably a relative or friend of your future wife, so make them feel welcome.

The minute I heard my first love story, I started looking for you, not knowing how blind that was. Lovers don't finally meet somewhere – they're in each other all along.

RUMI

OFFICIAL BUSINESS

When you talk to the officiant before the formal proceedings begin, make sure you raise any last-minute concerns about the order of events, the vows, the rings or the music. They will be able to put your mind at ease, and chatting to them informally first will make the wedding itself feel that much more intimate and relaxed.

BEFORE THE CEREMONY

⬧ Sip bottled water and have breath mints to hand before the ceremony starts, especially if it's a hot day. Mints are preferable to gum because you won't find yourself unintentionally chewing as your bride walks down the aisle.

⬧ Make sure your groomsmen earn their keep by handing out programmes and ushering people to their seats. They can also be responsible for fielding questions from other people at the venue.

Happiness, not in another place but this place… Not for another hour but this hour.

WALT WHITMAN

STAND TALL

Once you've made your way into position for the start of the ceremony, follow these steps so you don't look like you're having second thoughts.

◇ Stay seated until you're told that your bride-to-be is nearly ready to make her entrance.

◇ If you do want to stand, try to plant your feet with weight distributed evenly on both feet.

◇ Don't keep looking to the back of the room – it will make you look nervous and uncomfortable.

◇ Chat quietly with your groomsmen, but try not to be too boisterous.

◇ Subtly check your fly is closed.

◇ Traditionally, the groom doesn't turn to see the bride until she is standing beside him at the front, but if you choose to break with tradition, stick with your choice and watch her walk the entire way to meet you.

DON'T FORGET...

◇ Because you arrive first, you can see to it that everything is just as it should be. If your bride planned most of the wedding, get instructions from her ahead of time as to what should be in place so you know what to expect and so you can fix any last-minute problems before she shows up.

*Never tell a secret to a bride
or a groom; wait until they
have been married longer.*

E. W. HOWE

DISASTER DODGER

There's nothing worse than offending one of your bride's relatives before the wedding has even begun. Make sure you are always with your best man and tell him there are a few relatives whose names you're a bit iffy on. If someone comes over to wish you well before the ceremony, assuming that you know who they are when actually you don't, introduce your best man immediately in an agreed way so he will know to ask the person's name, avoiding any embarrassment.

YOUR NOTES

....
....
....
....
....
....
....
....
....
....
....
....
....
....
....
....
....

YOUR NOTES

....
....
....
....
....
....
....
....
....
....
....
....
....
....
....

POMP AND
CEREMONY

No matter what happens, you will
remember this part of the day for
the rest of your life: the vows, the
music, signing the register, walking
down the aisle as a married couple
– here's how to do it all with ease.

RESPECTING THE VENUE

Weddings are celebratory affairs, but they are also serious matters – both legally and/or spiritually. Everyone's views differ, but it is often the bride and groom who set the tone for how everyone else behaves. If you're marrying in a place of worship, respect the space you're in and encourage your guests to do the same. If you want a more relaxed approach, it might be advisable to be married in a non-religious setting.

*Marriage is a commitment;
a decision to do, all through
life, that which will express
your love for one's spouse.*

HERMAN H. KIEVAL

KEEPING IT TOGETHER

◇ Look into your bride's eyes when she reaches the front of your wedding venue – the whole atmosphere will be overwhelming, but the familiarity you share will help calm both your nerves.

◇ If you are doing a reading, remember to take slow, deep breaths, and speak loudly and clearly so all of your guests can enjoy it.

◇ Make sure you know which finger
   is the ring finger, and when it comes
   to that part of the ceremony, gently
   place it on rather than forcing it.

◇ A great way to mark your relationship
   with your new father-in-law is to
   acknowledge him after he's walked
   his daughter down the aisle, either
   with a hug, a handshake or a smile.

*This done, he took the bride
about the neck; and kiss'd her
lips with such a clamorous
smack, that, at the parting,
all the church did echo.*

WILLIAM SHAKESPEARE

You don't marry the person
you can live with… you
marry the person you
can't live without.

ANONYMOUS

DON'T FORGET...

Kissing for the first time as a married couple can cause problems for some. These following pointers will ensure your smooch goes swimmingly.

◇ Grab hold of each other and get close – you're married now, so there doesn't need to be a big gap between you.

◇ No sudden movements – you don't want to butt heads, teeth or noses, so go in nice and slow.

◇ Keep your eyes closed while you kiss – it will look better in the photos.

◇ Don't practise beforehand – the best kisses are the most natural ones.

◇ Remember where you are and who you're kissing in front of. Be it in a church, in front of your grandmother or the officiant, remember to keep it PG – X-rated kisses are what the honeymoon is for.

VOWS WITH POW

◇ If you are repeating standard vows, make sure you take your time to listen to the words the officiant is saying – these are the promises you're making to your partner, and you want to mean them, rather than robotically regurgitate them.

◇ If you're making additional personal vows, it's a good idea to have them written down – ask your best man to hold on to them and pass the paper to you at the appropriate moment.

◇ Look into each other's eyes, even if you're reading vows.

◇ If your voice starts to waver or even if you begin to cry, take a second to gather yourself, rather than mumbling through the rest of your vows.

*Marriage is the golden
ring in a chain whose
beginning is a glance and
whose ending is eternity.*

KAHLIL GIBRAN

My love has placed
her little hand
With noble faith in mine,
And vowed that wedlock's
sacred band
Our nature shall entwine.
My love has sworn,
with sealing kiss,
With me to live – to die;
I have at last my
nameless bliss:
As I love – loved am I!

CHARLOTTE BRONTË

DISASTER DODGER

The signing of the register is an important part of the wedding ceremony – officially marking its place in the history books. Make sure there's no awkward confusion by asking friends or relatives in advance if they will sign it for you. This will also prevent anyone being offended on the day for not being asked, causing potential arguments.

YOUR NOTES

....
....
....
....
....
....
....
....
....
....
....
....
....
....
....

YOUR NOTES

....

....

....

....

....

....

....

....

....

....

....

....

....

....

....

SAY CHEESE!

*You've gone to all that trouble
to look rather dapper, and your
bride is as beautiful as the day
you met her, if not more. Now
it's time to make sure you have
the ultimate keepsake from the
day – a wonderful wedding album
full of fantastic photographs.*

GETTING THE MOST FROM YOUR PHOTOS

◇ Be sure to get any photographs that include your guests out of the way first, so they can get on with enjoying the champagne and canapés while you are whisked off for a snapping session with your photographer.

◇ Make sure a trusted friend or relative is on hand with a pre-discussed list of all the various photograph groupings you would like. Although it's likely you will have discussed these with your photographer beforehand, a list will make sure no friends or relatives are left out.

◇ Smiling for all those photos could leave your jaw a little sore. Relax your expression after every few photos to avoid face ache and unnatural smiles.

◇ Make sure you're not photographed in direct sunlight – squinting is definitely not your best look.

◇ Don't obsess over how the pictures will turn out – trust your photographer and their experience and enjoy staring lovingly into your other half's eyes.

◇ Why not take a few 'selfies' of you and your other half in between the photographer setting up shots for some extra-special memories you can post online throughout the day.

The whole point of taking pictures is so that you don't have to explain things with words.

ELLIOTT ERWITT

*Success in marriage does
not come merely through
finding the right mate, but
through being the right mate.*

BARNETT BRICKNER

POSING MASTERCLASS

◇ Natural smiles are best, so let the photographer make you laugh.

◇ Make sure you remove all items from your pockets before the photographer starts – keys, phone, wallet, etc. No one wants to see unsightly bulges in their wedding pictures.

◇ Don't thrust out your chest to try and make yourself look bigger – it will only serve to emphasise that paunch. Instead, put your arms behind your back, pull your shoulders back and relax.

◇ Find useful places for your hands to go so they don't look silly – in your pockets, round your wife's waist, holding her hand, etc.

◇ You look dapper, so feel it too and your confidence and joy will shine through in your pictures.

*There are no bad pictures;
that's just how your face
looks sometimes.*

ABRAHAM LINCOLN

What I like about photographs is that they capture a moment that's gone forever, impossible to reproduce.

KARL LAGERFELD

DON'T FORGET...

Have the following items to hand while you're having your photos taken:

◇ Tissues (in case you get emotional, or if you get 'something' in your eye)

◇ Comb (if your hair requires it)

◇ Your best man if you want someone to help hold things for you and your bride (like her bag, your jackets, etc.)

◇ A glass of champagne.

*A photograph can be an
instant of life captured
for eternity that will never
cease looking back at you.*

<small>Brigitte Bardot</small>

DISASTER DODGER

If your bride is fussing over you before and during the photographs, let her. She wants you both to look your best, because she knows she will be enjoying these pictures for the rest of her life. If anything, it's evidence of how much she loves you. Let her fuss and adjust – you know you'll be grateful to look good in the long run.

YOUR NOTES

....
....
....
....
....
....
....
....
....
....
....
....
....
....
....
....
....
....

YOUR NOTES

....
....
....
....
....
....
....
....
....
....
....
....
....
....

A GRAND
RECEPTION

*Some grooms spend hours and
hours poring over wedding
blogs to find the perfect venues,
decorations and dinner menu
for their big day. Some… do not.
Whether you're satisfied with your
work or completely surprised, this
will be an evening to remember
for the rest of your life.*

PRIORITISING YOUR TIME

◇ With all the friends and family
  around it's easy to spend your entire
  day chatting with everyone but your
  other half. Make sure you find each
  other throughout the night and not
  just to pose for cameras.

◇ Depending on how many guests are at your wedding, you will have an awful lot of people to meet and greet. Spend more time with your guests at their tables, rather than in a formal receiving line, by starting the dinner first and then greeting people one table at a time between courses. This gives them the opportunity to congratulate you, take your picture and see your outfits up close without the pressure of a moving line.

*After all, there's something
about a wedding gown,
prettier than in any other
gown in the world.*

Douglas William Herrold

YOUR BEAUTIFUL BRIDE

◇ As much as you might want to have a quick make-out session in the car, don't leave your guests waiting too long – people will be hungry and don't want to hang around for hours.

◇ If your bride's opted for a big, beautiful ballgown, she might need to move a little slower than normal and a bit of help manoeuvring her dress around the space.

◇ Be sure to comment on how fantastic everything looks and shower your bride with compliments – after all, she worked really hard to pull this wedding off.

DON'T FORGET...

A good wedding planner will make sure all the elements of your wedding come together and are appreciated by your guests. In the absence of one, let your wife relax and enjoy herself, and check off the following when you arrive at your reception venue:

◇ Have all the decorations/flowers/ furniture you ordered arrived?

◇ Have all the appropriate place cards, party favours and centrepieces been added to the tables?

◇ Is the seating plan positioned where guests can see it?

◇ Have the tables been named or numbered correctly?

◇ Do the guests know the bar policy?

◇ Is there a clear timetable for the staff regarding drinks, food and entertainment?

◇ If you are having any entertainment, has it arrived? Are there any problems?

◇ What is the schedule for any musical elements to the reception?

FOOD FOR THOUGHT

◇ Remember that if you're planning on showing your wife a good time in the bridal suite, go easy on those triple servings – you don't want to end the night in a food coma.

◇ Enjoy the food, but eat gracefully with a large napkin across your lap to defend yourself against unsightly stains.

◈ Save room for cake! Your cake is never going to taste as good as on your wedding day. If you're a dessert person, this might be something you spent hours picking out so make sure you're not too stuffed to enjoy some!

◈ Follow each glass of alcohol with a full glass of water to stay hydrated and to ward off the more unglamorous effects of drinking.

So I commended enjoyment, because a man has nothing better under the sun than to eat, drink and be merry.

ECCLESIASTES 8:15, THE BIBLE

DISASTER DODGER

More and more couples are choosing outside wedding reception venues, which can be magical and make for great photos. What doesn't look so great, however, is sunburn. If you're prone to burning, make sure you've brought a high-factor sunscreen with you to reapply throughout the day, otherwise your missus will be asking you to Photoshop red blotches out of your wedding album.

*It is not the quantity
of the meat, but the
cheerfulness of the guests,
which makes the feast.*

EDWARD HYDE

*I dreamed of a wedding
of elaborate elegance; a
church filled with flowers
and friends. I asked him
what kind of wedding he
wished for; he said one that
would make me his wife.*

ANONYMOUS

YOUR NOTES

....
....
....
....
....
....
....
....
....
....
....
....
....
....
....

YOUR NOTES

....
....
....
....
....
....
....
....
....
....
....
....
....
....

TOASTS AND CAKE

*You survived the walk down
the aisle, the first kiss, the grand
entrance – but now comes the real
test: the speeches. Soak up the love
and pride of your guests and the
sweetness of your cake, and be
prepared for the occasional cringe!*

KEEPING THE TOASTS IN CHECK

◇ Have those people giving the speeches stand beside the cake table – it makes for a lovely backdrop for photographs, and means that the whole room can be addressed, including those at the top table.

◇ It's a good idea to keep speeches to a minimum, and a time limit, otherwise guests can become restless. Break speeches up with dinner courses, music or a slideshow.

◇ Cut your cake immediately after the speeches when you have everyone's attention and all your guests are still present.

THE BEST MAN'S SPEECH

◇ The key to good wedding toasts is
timing and organisation. If your best
man is running things, try to keep
an eye on how much he's drinking
during dinner to avoid the toasts
turning into a second stag night. A
good way to avoid this is to make
sure the toasts take place fairly early
on so there's less chance of a blotto
best man.

⬦ If he remains sober enough, your best man is going to deliver a speech. If he keeps it tame and teary, make a special mention of him in your own toast. If he decides to leave taste and decency at the door, keep a cool head, blush approvingly and recount an equally shameful story about him to the bridesmaids at the bar, especially if he thought he might be getting lucky later on.

THE FIRST DANCE

If you're having a first dance, wait until your caterer has cut up the wedding cake and served it to your guests, that way they have something to nibble on while you're strutting your stuff.

Don't fancy having your dancing skills on display? Avoid the first dance by inviting everyone onto the dance floor immediately after the cutting of the cake.

*Let us celebrate the occasion
with wine and sweet words.*

PLAUTUS

DON'T FORGET...

It's traditional for the groom to say a few words, and even if you're the shy type it will mean a lot to the bride and her parents, so brush up on your public-speaking skills and remember to thank the following people:

◈ Both sets of parents, where appropriate, especially those who contributed to the cost of the wedding

◇ The maid of honour, best man, bridesmaids and groomsmen, and give them any token gifts you have bought

◇ Any flower girls or pageboys

◇ Your wife's family for being so welcoming and for coming to the wedding

◇ Any other friends or family who have contributed significantly to the wedding (e.g. making the cake, doing the flowers, etc.).

In all of the wedding cake,
hope is the sweetest of plums.

D<small>OUGLAS</small> J<small>ERROLD</small>

I was the best man at a wedding one time... If I'm the best man, why is she marrying him?

JERRY SEINFELD

SURPRISE, SURPRISE!

◇ If you're planning on surprising your bride on the big day, make sure you squeeze it into the proceedings seamlessly (after the toasts and cake-cutting is a good idea). Wait till your guests are eating cake and you'll have their undivided attention.

◇ Why not showcase your sexy dance moves with a choreographed performance with your mates, or sing her a song you wrote especially for the wedding?

◇ If you fancy blowing your wife's mind, hire her favourite band to play (and tell her they were unavailable in the build-up to the day) or pay for a celebrity she loves to record a personalised message of congratulations.

◇ A really personal surprise sure to melt any bride's heart would be a video montage of photographs of the two of you throughout your relationship, with her favourite song playing in the background.

*A wedding anniversary
is the celebration of love,
trust, partnership, tolerance
and tenacity. The order
varies for any given year.*

PAUL SWEENEY

DISASTER DODGER

When it comes to the age-old tradition of feeding each other from the first slice of wedding cake, it's easy to get carried away (after a few glasses of champagne) and want to initiate a food fight with your hot new wife. She might be all smiles now, but be warned – very few brides want their make-up ruined and cake in their hair, so stick to a more girl-friendly approach if you want to stay in her good books.

Cakes are special… Every celebration ends with something sweet, a cake, and people remember. It's all about the memories.

BUDDY VALASTRO

YOUR NOTES

....

....

....

....

....

....

....

....

....

....

....

....

....

....

YOUR NOTES

....
....
....
....
....
....
....
....
....
....
....
....
....
....
....

PARTY TIME

Toasts and treats done, it's time to gossip, gulp and gyrate the night away with friends and family, and – most importantly – your sexy new wife!

*Celebrate the happiness that
friends are always giving,
make every day a holiday
and celebrate just living.*

SYDNEY SMITH

MAKING YOUR EXIT

You don't want to be one of the last people on the tiles, but equally you don't want to miss out on the party you're paying for. Have your mode of transportation ready to pick you up about an hour before the planned end of your reception. Then you have the option to have a proper send-off with all your guests before they leave, or stay a little longer if the party is going strong.

Music expresses that which cannot be put into words and that which cannot remain silent.

VICTOR HUGO

SHARING
THE LOAD

Make sure you and your bride aren't left doing any of the heavy lifting at the end of the night. Arrange for family members or friends to take charge of transporting any wedding gifts, centrepieces and leftover wedding cake, so you can head to your post-nuptial love nest worry-free.

THE LIFE OF THE PARTY

◇ If you have extra guests arriving just for the evening, make sure you go out of your way to greet them and socialise with them on the dance floor.

◇ If the DJ isn't playing the music you agreed on, or you think your guests would appreciate something different, don't be afraid to ask – it's your party!

◇ Golden oldies and dorky dance moves may seem cheesy, but they'll get everyone on their feet feeling comfortable and having fun.

◇ If you've organised any late-night food, such as a finger buffet or a food truck, make sure your guests know about it, otherwise you could end up leaving with your wife and a whole car-full of sausage rolls.

*Those who danced were
thought to be quite insane
by those who could
not hear the music.*

ANGELA MONET

Love is the master key that opens the gates of happiness.

OLIVER WENDELL HOLMES SR

DON'T FORGET...

◇ Weddings can turn into quite raucous affairs, depending on the crowd – but that's not for everyone. Be considerate of your in-laws and keep an eye on your friends' behaviour if you want to make a good impression.

◇ Hanging out with your mates is a blast, but you do it every Saturday night. Make sure you're including other people in the fun, especially those who might have come on their own.

◇ Stay sober enough to say goodbye to anyone who heads off early and so that you can carry your bride over the threshold of your hotel room.

*Opportunity dances
with those already on
the dance floor.*

H. Jackson Brown Jr

*Dancing is the poetry
of the foot.*

JOHN DRYDEN

DISASTER DODGER

If there are a number of children attending your wedding, it's a good idea to start the dance proceedings with more kid-friendly songs (or even allocate a separate space in the venue for a kids' party). This way they'll tire themselves out early and avoid being accidental victims of a crowded dance floor later in the night.

YOUR NOTES

....
....
....
....
....
....
....
....
....
....
....
....
....
....
....
....

YOUR NOTES

....
....
....
....
....
....
....
....
....
....
....
....
....
....

HONEYMOONERS

Your wedding was the day of your dreams, and now that it's all over you'll likely feel exhausted, poor and perhaps a little deflated. These tips will make sure you have a spring in your step long after the honeymoon suite.

LIFE GOES ON

◇ For some couples who already live together, own a house, have children and share bank accounts, not much will change after the wedding is over, but it's still important to make time to celebrate this exciting transition in your lives as a couple. Organise a dinner party with close friends, book your honeymoon or a weekend away, and start making plans for your home and your future.

◇ Boring as it may seem after planning the party of the century, you might want to start thinking about your financial situation: bank accounts, life insurance, pensions and your savings. You also might want to write a will (if you already have individual wills these should be rewritten now you're married). These might be things you've avoided before but there's no time like the present to cement yourself as a married couple.

Chains do not hold a marriage together. It is threads, hundreds of tiny threads, which sew people together through the years.

<small>SIMONE SIGNORET</small>

*A happy marriage is a
long conversation which
always seems too short.*

ANDRÉ MAUROIS

THE CALM AFTER THE STORM

◇ Don't panic if you don't have sex on your wedding night – it's quite common to pass out after such a long day and all that partying. It doesn't mean you love each other any less, and remember: there's always the morning after and the rest of your lives for the good stuff.

◇ If you're not leaving for a honeymoon immediately, enjoy a few days together relaxing, taking long walks and steamy showers, and avoid feeling the post-wedding blues by reminiscing about the big day and opening your gifts.

DON'T FORGET...

If you weren't heavily involved in planning the wedding, see if you can make up for it by ticking off as many of the post-party to-dos as possible:

◇ Paying any invoices for wedding goods and services

◇ Having your wedding outfits dry-cleaned

◇ Helping your wife to change her name, if she has chosen to, or changing your names together, with all the relevant organisations (banks, credit card companies, doctors, the tax office, your driver's licence and passport)

◇ Packing for the honeymoon and making last-minute activity bookings

◇ Chasing up the photographer and/ or videographer for the pictures and video from the wedding.

HOW TO HONEYMOON

◇ Don't put too much pressure on the honeymoon to be the most amazing time of your lives. Chances are it will be fantastic, but too much pressure for lots of sex, exceptional hotels and perfect weather can cause disappointment.

◇ Mention you're on your honeymoon everywhere you go – you never know what freebies are on offer to lovebirds.

◇ If your wife wants a bit of alone time on the honeymoon, she hasn't gone off you already – it's healthy to spend a bit of the holiday apart, especially if she found planning the wedding stressful. Do the same by getting into a good book, going for a run or chatting with the locals.

◇ Book a special activity in advance to surprise your wife (e.g. scuba-diving or salsa lessons, or a romantic helicopter ride).

THANKING
YOUR GUESTS

◇ Create an invite-only file-sharing depository online using a site like Flickr or Dropbox for all your nearest and dearest to upload and share any pictures they took.

◇ If you have a wedding website, send out a general message to everyone thanking them for coming.

*Marriage should be a
duet – when one sings,
the other claps.*

JOE MURRAY

DISASTER DODGER

Don't start married life on the wrong foot by not helping out and doing your part. Create a spreadsheet to keep track of all the wedding gifts, buy some thank-you cards and a bottle of wine, and have a quiet night in on the sofa writing them together. Just be sure not to squish your hard work if things start heating up between the two of you.

*A successful marriage
requires falling in love
many times, always with
the same person.*

MIGNON MCLAUGHLIN

YOUR NOTES

....
....
....
....
....
....
....
....
....
....
....
....
....
....
....

YOUR NOTES

....
....
....
....
....
....
....
....
....
....
....
....
....
....
....

If you're interested in finding out more about our books, find us on Facebook at **Summersdale Publishers** and follow us on Twitter at **@Summersdale**.

www.summersdale.com